YELLOWSTONE FIRES
Flames and Rebirth

DOROTHY HINSHAW PATENT

photos by William Muñoz and Others

Holiday House / New York

Library of Congress Cataloging-in-Publication Data

Patent, Dorothy Hinshaw.
    Yellowstone fires / written by Dorothy Hinshaw Patent ; Photographs by William Muñoz and others. — 1st ed.
        p.   cm.
    Summary: Describes the massive forest fires that burned almost one million acres of Yellowstone National Park in 1988 and the effects, both positive and negative, on the ecology of the forest there.
    ISBN 0-8234-0807-8
    1. Forest fires — Yellowstone National Park — Juvenile literature.   2. Forest fires — Government policy — Yellowstone National Park — Juvenile literature.   3. Yellowstone National Park — Juvenile literature.   4. Fire ecology — Yellowstone National Park — Juvenile literature.   [1. Forest fires — Yellowstone National Park.   2. Fire ecology.   3. Ecology.   4. Yellowstone National Park.   5. National parks and reserves.] I. Muñoz, William, ill.   II. Title.
SD421.32.Y45P38   1990   89-24544   CIP   AC   574.5'222 — dc20

To the children of today and the future,
who will watch Yellowstone change and renew.

D. H. P. and W. M.

The author and photographer wish to thank
Sandy Robinson, Mary Ann Davis, and Jim Peaco
from the National Park Service at
Yellowstone for their help.

CHAPTER ONE

Setting the Stage

In the summer of 1988, fires in Yellowstone National Park made news across the nation. Headlines screamed that the park had burned up, that nothing was left. Luckily, those stories weren't true. Yellowstone is alive and well. Much of the park did burn, but nature has been rebuilding. What really happened that summer? Why in Yellowstone? And what can we expect for the future of the park?

Clouds of smoke from the North Fork Fire, one of the biggest of the 1988 Yellowstone fires.

Forests for Burning

Yellowstone will heal because it is used to fire. In our lives, we normally think in terms of a few years or at most a human lifetime. But the cycles of nature often are longer than that. In 1988, Yellowstone hadn't had huge fires since the early 1700s, although some large ones burned in the 1800s. The forests were ready to burn again.

The lodgepole pine forests of Yellowstone are adapted to fire.

Eighty percent of the park's trees are lodgepole pines—miles and miles of them. Lodgepoles grow quickly. But they don't live very long compared to some other trees. After about two hundred years, the trees in a lodgepole forest begin to die. The dead and dying trees are blown down in storms. As more and more trees fall, young ones grow up to take their place, and the floor of the forest keeps collecting wood from fallen trees.

In areas where lots of rain falls, the dead wood on the forest floor is attacked by fungus and bacteria which break it down. But in dry forests, like those of Yellowstone, most of the dead trees stay where they fall. Just like in a fireplace, this wood acts as fuel for fire. A lodgepole forest that is three hundred years old has so much dead wood that walking through it is difficult. There are logs to climb over everywhere.

Old lodgepole forests are marked by dead wood on the forest floor and by standing dead trees, often killed by beetles.
DOROTHY H. PATENT

Rain and Drought

Normally, the Yellowstone area gets most of its moisture in the wintertime, from snow. When spring comes, the snow melts, soaking the ground, and plants grow. In normal years, some rain also comes to Yellowstone in June, July, and August.

It took hundreds of years to set the stage for the 1988 fires. Much of the forest grew for over two hundred years without really big fires, and the dead wood built up on the forest floor. Then, for six years in the 1980s, snowfall was light during the winter, making drought conditions build.

In April and May of 1988, much more than the normal amount of rain fell. This helped the small trees and other plants between the mature forest trees grow well. When June came, the park managers were not worried. They had no reason to suspect that June would only have 20 percent of its normal rainfall and that almost no rain would fall in early July. They didn't know that 1988 would turn out to be the driest summer ever recorded since the park was established 116 years earlier.

When forests and meadows are dry, they burn easily.

CHAPTER TWO

Should We Put Out Fires?

Until 1972, all fires that started in national parks and that could be reached were fought. People saw fires as bad. After all, they killed trees and made ugly scars on the land. But as scientists learned more and more about nature, they realized that fire has its place. They learned that when dry northern forests go too long without fire, more and more nutrients are locked up in the dead and living trees. There aren't enough nutrients available for the trees to grow and stay healthy. It's as if the forests were starving.

The 1988 fires helped open up meadows in which elk could graze.

Fire–A Part of Nature

When Yellowstone was founded over a hundred years ago, there were more open meadows than there are today. The lodgepole forests have been taking over the open land, leaving less room for grazing animals like elk to feed. Fires help maintain meadows by burning the small trees growing along their edges.

Fire causes lodgepole cones to open, releasing the seeds of the new forest.

In addition, many kinds of plants and animals are adapted to survive or even thrive after fires. Lodgepoles, for example, produce two kinds of cones. One kind opens by itself, but the other is sealed by sticky resin. The seeds inside these special cones can stay alive for years, waiting to be released by the heat of a fire. Temperatures over 113 degrees Fahrenheit will melt the resin, and the cones will open. Then the seeds are scattered over the burned ground to reseed the forest. In areas like Yellowstone, where fire is a natural part of nature's cycles, most of the lodgepole's cones are the sealed type.

Fireweed, which produces beautiful bright pink flowers, doesn't grow well in the shade. It survives in small numbers around the edges of forests. When fire burns the trees, fireweed survives because its underground stems are protected from the heat. Its dandelion-like seeds are also carried by the wind into burned areas. The year after a fire, fireweed can create a brilliant carpet of flowers among the blackened remains of the trees.

Fireweed thrives after fires or in disturbed areas, including along roadsides.

A Change of Policy

Once scientists understood that fire is an important natural force with healthy effects, they decided that not all fires should be fought after all. In 1972, a new policy began. If a fire was started by lightning in a national forest or a national park, it wasn't put out unless it caused a threat to private property or to buildings. In national forests, the needs of the timber industry, which cuts trees for wood and wood products, were also considered. The fires were watched closely. If they might become dangerous, they were stopped. Any fires caused by people were put out right away. The forest and park managers felt this new policy would help keep the parks and forests more natural.

This natural fire policy worked well in Yellowstone. From 1972 to 1987, 233 lightning fires were left alone. Of these, 205 covered less than one acre before going out naturally. The largest of the other 28 fires burned only 7,396 acres, less than 1/300th of the land in the park.

Lightning strikes cause many fires, but most burn out quickly.

CHAPTER THREE

Yellowstone Aflame

A number of fires started in Yellowstone and in the surrounding forests during June of 1988. The park itself lies at the center of a region called the "Yellowstone Ecosystem," or "Greater Yellowstone Area." Besides Yellowstone, the ecosystem includes Grand Teton National Park and the lands of several national forests. No one can hunt, cut trees for wood, or mine in a national park. But in the forests, these activities can take place.

Lightning sparked a fire on June 14 in the Storm Creek area of Custer National Forest north of the park. Officials decided to let it burn, since it was far from towns, homesites, or ranches. No one thought this fire would become destructive. But as the summer went on, it became one of the most dangerous of all, growing to more than 95,000 acres.

Grand Teton National Park

Fires started in the park itself as well. Many were allowed to burn, and most went out quickly by themselves before covering an acre. But by July 15, things began to look bad. The expected rainfall hadn't arrived, and the forests were very dry. About 8,000 acres in the park had burned. And winds were making the fires grow dangerously fast.

The North Fork Fire burns just a few miles south of Mammoth Hot Springs on September 10, the same day Mammoth was evacuated.   JIM PEACO/NATIONAL PARK SERVICE

Trying to Stop the Fires

Less than a week later, on July 21, park officials decided to fight all fires in the park. By then, almost 17,000 acres had already burned. The next day, a cigarette left by a careless wood gatherer started a fire in the North Fork area of the Targhee National Forest just west of the park. Fire fighters began to fight it the same day. Meanwhile, in the northeast part of the park, two fires that started the second week in July joined to become the Clover-Mist Fire.

Unfortunately, the wind whipped up on July 23, two days after the decision to fight all fires. The combination of the wind and the dry conditions was too much for the fire fighters. The North Fork Fire, less than 30 acres when reported, grew to 500 acres before it was a day old, despite the fact that smoke jumpers–parachuting fire fighters–were sent in right away. The wind also carried bits of burning material such as pine cones, called "firebrands," as far as a half mile in front of the fire. By the end of July 23, the North Fork Fire had consumed 1,300 acres. Other fires expanded during the winds as well, including one that grew from 160 acres to 2,000 in just two days. Officials didn't know it at the time, but the uncontrolled burning of Yellowstone had begun.

Black Saturday

In early August, fire experts from around the country gathered in Yellowstone to discuss the future of the fires. They decided that conditions would not allow more than 200,000 acres to burn, even if rain didn't come. How wrong they were. By August 12, 201,000 acres had already burned, and that was really just the beginning.

August 20, 1988, will always be known as Black Saturday in Yellowstone. Throughout the park, eighty-mile-per-hour, hurricane-force gusts of wind whipped up almost every fire that was burning. The North Fork Fire moved into an area where strong winds had blown down trees in 1984. With so much fuel, the fire burned especially hot and left a dead-looking landscape behind. The Storm Creek Fire, which had almost died out, came to life and moved ten miles in three hours. The Hellroaring Fire, which had started only five days earlier north of the park, grew to cover over 30,000 acres. Altogether, 165,000 acres burned on that one day alone. Black Saturday taught the experts that they could predict nothing about the extraordinary fires of 1988.

Smoke from the fires often blocked out the sun.

The North Fork Fire burned through an area where strong winds blew down trees in 1984, and most of the dead trees burned up. Now the forest can regrow.

CHAPTER FOUR

Fighting the Fires

As the fires burned, they threatened more than just Yellowstone's forests. The Clover-Mist and Storm Creek fires both came within a few miles of Cooke City and Silver Gate, Montana, two communities near the northeast corner of the park. Luckily, fire fighters stopped them from consuming the towns. The North Fork Fire threatened Canyon Village, inside the park. On August 24, five hundred tourists and employees were evacuated as the fire came within five miles of the area.

The Fires Spread

The North Fork Fire kept getting bigger and threatened the town of West Yellowstone, Montana. For days, bulldozers tore away trees and bushes to stop the fire before it could reach the town as ashes rained onto its streets.

The most famous siege came at Old Faithful, the popular geyser area. Geysers don't burn. But buildings do, and Old Faithful Inn, built in 1903, is a beautiful historic structure. In early September, an incredible fire storm, with raging flames consuming entire living trees and everything in their path, came perilously close to the inn. Fortunately, the inn was saved by a new sprinkler system on its roof and a shift in the wind. But twenty smaller buildings in the area, including tourist cabins, were burned up.

The North Fork Fire approaches Old Faithful in this photo taken from the roof of the inn. JEFF HENRY/NATIONAL PARK SERVICE

Old Faithful still performs on schedule, and the historic inn still takes in visitors. Only the forest beyond shows the effects of fire.

Fire fighters had all they could do to protect the towns and visitor areas in the park from the fires. The second week of September, the North Fork Fire threatened Mammoth Hot

Springs, the headquarters of the park. But on September 11, snow fell, quieting the fires. Nature had done what tremendous human effort couldn't, even after $120 million was spent. That snow was the beginning of a season of damp fall weather, and the worst of the fires were over.

How the Fires Were Fought

Many methods were used to fight the fires. Trained fire fighters came from California, Alabama, Florida, and other states all over the country. They were joined by soldiers and local volunteers. Fire fighting is hard work. Heavy axes called "Pulaskis" are used to cut away trees. Teams of fire fighters also use their Pulaskis to dig up the ground, breaking up the surface vegetation to slow the fires. At first, bulldozers weren't used in the park, since they create so much damage to the ground. But when buildings were threatened, the bulldozers did their share. When the fire storms were raging, however, they raced across bulldozer lines and rivers, and spread by firebrands carried on the wind. During the worst of the fires, in the middle of the day, the sky was as dark as sunset. The heavy smoke made it hard to breathe or see, and the heat was intense.

Fire retardant is dropped by low-flying planes to slow down the flames.
MICHAEL MUNOZ

Airplanes dropped loads of chemicals that slow down fires, and helicopters dipped buckets into lakes and rivers, dumping the water on the flames. Where the wind direction allowed, "backfires" were lit on purpose in front of the fire to destroy its fuel. But the big fires were too powerful to be contained.

Uncontrollable Burning

The Yellowstone fires were awesome. No matter how hard they tried, humans could not stop them. The raging winds helped the flames race across the landscape. When firebrands hit dry timber, entire trees burst into flames. The trees were dry, and lots of dead wood lay on the forest floor. Trees killed by bark beetles stood in some areas, perfect fuel for flames. The rain didn't fall, and the trees were tinder-dry. These conditions are perfect for fires to crown. When that happens, the flames consume the entire tree. The tops, or crowns, of even the living trees become engulfed in flame. These are called "canopy fires," since they burn the branches that form a covering, or canopy, over the forest. Canopy fires are especially difficult to fight. The heat from the intense fire increases the wind, and the wind carries firebrands as far as two miles to unburned areas, starting still more fires.

The fires burned most of the dead wood on the forest floor, as well as burning the trees.

The canopy fires of 1988 were an awesome sight.

Canopy fires can move very quickly, frustrating efforts to stop them. And firebrands can start fires behind the fire fighters, making their work especially dangerous. They could become quickly surrounded by flames and trapped.

CHAPTER FIVE

Aftermath

Snow and rain stopped the worst of the fires in September. But here and there, fires smoldered and occasionally flamed up until November. By the time it was all over, eight huge fires had covered almost half of the park. The northwestern corner was hardest hit. But the southeast and northeast corners were also badly burned. Altogether, eleven major fires had

While the canopy fires captured the headlines, surface fires that cleared out the undergrowth without killing the trees burned through much of the park.

burned in the Greater Yellowstone Area, fought by 9,500 fire fighters. In the wake of the fires, officials decided temporarily to fight all fires in national parks and forests until a new policy that coordinated fire management plans in parks and the surrounding national forests could be worked out.

How Much Burned?

Now it was time to see how much damage the fires had really caused. Television and newspaper stories made it sound as if Yellowstone was destroyed. But it wasn't. Many of the fires had not crowned and become canopy fires. They had just burned along the forest floor and not killed the trees. Other fires had burned over meadows and sagebrush.

Meadows as well as forests burned in 1988.

A burned marsh in fall 1988.

Altogether, just under 990,000 acres in the 2.2-million-acre park had suffered some burning. Of this, 57 percent were canopy fires and 38 percent surface fires. The rest burned over grasslands and meadows. In the Greater Yellowstone Area, 1.4 million acres were affected by the fires.

Park researchers looked at the soil to see if plant roots and seeds had been killed. Fortunately, even in the worst burn areas, the roots of bushes were still alive below the ground. Lodgepole cones opened by the fire had scattered seeds all over the forest floor. They would grow to form the new forest.

The large animals in the park showed little concern for the fires burning near them.

Fire and Wildlife

Many people worried about the park animals during the fires. Would they be burned? It is difficult to count animals killed in fires, especially small ones. But the bodies of fewer than three hundred large animals, mostly elk, were found out of the thousands that roam the park. When the fire approached, bison, elk, deer, and pronghorn just moved away. Throughout the park, animals grazed near the fires. They were more disturbed by the noisy helicopters that flew overhead than by the flames.

Some birds benefited during the fires. They hunted for food near the edges of the fires, feeding on small animals that were escaping. Young bald eagles had already flown from their nests before the fires threatened them, so they escaped. One osprey nest was burned before the young could fly.

Strangely enough, more birds died on the roads than in the fires. Fire fighters drove many cars and trucks over park roads, often through thick smoke that made it difficult to see animals on the road. Grouse, owls, flickers, and hawks were killed in this way.

Animals like the coyote benefited from the fires.

Most of the fires created a mosaic of burned places, killed trees, and unburned areas. As time passes, these varied patches will result in a greater variety of habitats for the park's plants and animals.

Mosaic for Life

The way the fires burned—crowning in some areas and burning along the ground in others—has created a much more varied landscape than before the fires. Now patches of untouched mature forest stand next to completely blackened areas. Nearby, the forest floor of other stretches has been cleared by surface fires. This patchiness—called a mosaic—provides a greater variety of homes for both plants and animals. Some plants require lots of sunlight and can't grow under the trees. They will now be able to thrive in the burned areas. Large animals like deer and elk find it difficult to move through the dense cover of downed wood in the mature lodgepole forest. They will be able to use the newly opened areas much more easily.

CHAPTER SIX

The Future

Signs of renewal were already clear in the spring of 1989. Twenty kinds of grasses sprouted on the burned forest floor, mixed with flowers such as delicate shooting stars. The burned meadows grew more vigorously than before, with a healthy, deep green glow, nourished by the nitrogen and other nutrients released by the fires. The new growth is not only healthy and green, it actually contains more nutrients for the animals like elk that eat it. Grazers prefer the grass and other plants in recently burned areas, and it makes them healthier than grass in unburned meadows.

The lodgepole pine seeds covering the forest floor also began to grow into new trees that year. They were tiny and difficult to see, but they were there. By the end of the growing season, they had reached an inch and a half in height.

Between the new seedlings, the roots of bushes and shrubs had sent up new growth, giving the blackened forest some greenery.

A shooting star blooms in a burned meadow in the spring of 1989.

The fires burned the sagebrush, leaving more open space for grasses to thrive.

This aspen grove was spared during 1988. But in the long run, it probably would be healthier if it had burned so it could have sprouted vigorous new shoots.

Changes in Plants and Animals

The kinds of plants and animals that thrive in recently burned areas are different from those that prefer the old forest. For this reason, differences in the populations of plants and animals in Yellowstone should follow the fires. Aspen groves, which count on fires to keep them healthy, had been declining in the park. Park ecologists hope that now the groves will regain their strength. Willows should react in a similar way.

Small birds like warblers and sparrows should benefit from the more varied habitat that follows fire. Their numbers should increase. But other kinds, such as the goshawk, depend on the old growth and will be scarce in the burned areas. Plenty of unburned forest remains, however, to provide homes for such animals.

The Yellowstone elk herds should become much healthier than before. They can feast on the more nutritious grasses and enjoy eating the fireweed that is abundant following fire. With more open ground, there will be more grass and other sun-loving plants for the elk to eat.

Yellowstone bison like these will be healthier after eating the nutritious grass that follows fire.

As Time Goes On

The forest takes on a new look only three years after the fire. The old forest floor is totally green. The dead trees have lost their bark and look silver instead of black. The tiny new lodgepoles are about six inches tall.

Within ten years, the young trees will be tall enough to make the beginnings of a new green forest underneath the old silver one. Some of them may already be producing cones.

Fire encourages diversity in both plants and animals. The greatest number of species in a forest is found about twenty-five years after a fire. When the lodgepoles grow big enough that the canopy closes—forty to fifty years after the burn—the number of species drops.

Around 100 to 150 years after the forest has burned, the weak trees will begin to die and fall to the forest floor. The cycle will begin to turn back toward its beginning, with fuel for future forests starting to build up underneath the trees. And later on, probably sometime during the twenty-third century, the forests of Yellowstone will burn again.

Index

(Numbers in *italics* refer to pages with illustrations)

airplanes, 26, *26*
aspens, 37, *37*

backfires, 26
birds, 33, 38
bison, 32, *32*, *34*, *38*
Black Saturday, 20
bulldozers, 25

canopy fires, 27-28, *28*, 31
Canyon Village, 22
Clover-Mist Fire, 19, 22
Cooke City, Montana, 22
coyote, *33*
Custer National Forest, 16

deer, 32
drought, 8

elk, *11*, 32, 38

fighting fires, 25-26
fire ecology, 6-7, 10-13, 27, 34,
    35-39
fire management policy, 10, 14, 16,
    19, 30
fire retardant, 26, *26*
fireweed, 13, *13*
firebrands, 19, 27

Grand Teton National Park, 16, *17*

helicopters, 26, 32
Hellroaring Fire, 20

lightning fires, 14, *15*, 16
lodgepole pines, *6*, 7, *7*, 12, *12*, 35,
    39

Mammoth Hot Springs, 24-25
meadows, *9*, 11, *11*, *30*, 31, 35
mosiac burn, 34, *34*

national forests, 14, 16
national parks, 14, 16
North Fork Fire, *5*, *18*, 19, 20, *21*,
    22-25, *23*

Old Faithful, 23, *23*, *24*

pinecones, *12*, 12-13, 31, 39
pronghorn, 32
Pulaskis, 25

rain, 8, 29

shooting star, 35, *36*
Silver Gate, Montana, 22
smoke jumpers, 19
snow, 8, 25, 29
Storm Creek Fire, 16, 20, 22
surface fires, *29*, 30, 31

Targhee National Forest, 19

West Yellowstone, Montana, 22-23
willows, 37

Yellowstone Ecosystem, 16, 29-31